Myths of
Pre-Columbian
AMERICA

Anita Dalal

RSVP

RAINTREE
STECK-VAUGHN
PUBLISHERS
A Steck-Vaughn Company

Steck–Vaughn Company
First published 2001 by Raintree Steck-Vaughn Publishers, an imprint of Steck-Vaughn Company.
© 2002 Brown Partworks Limited

Library of Congress Cataloging-in-Publication Data
Dalal, Anita.
    Myths of pre-Columbian America / Anita Dalal.
        p. cm. -- (Mythic world)
    Includes bibliographical references and index.
    ISBN 0-7398-3193-3
     1. Aztec mythology--Juvenile literature. 2. Indian mythology--Latin America--Juvenile
literature. 3. Aztecs--Juvenile literature. [1. Aztecs--Folklore. 2. Incas--Folklore. 3. Mayas--Folklore.
4. Indians of Mexico--Folklore. 5. Indians of South America--Folklore. 6. Indians of Central America--
Folklore. 7. Folklore--Mexico. 8. Folklore--Peru. 9.Folklore--Central America.] I. Title. II. Series.

F1219.76.R45 D35 2001
398.2'089'97452--dc21

                                          2001019814
Printed and bound in the United States
1 2 3 4 5 6 7 8 9 0 IP 05 04 03 02 01

Series Consultant: C. Scott Littleton, Professor of Anthropology,
Occidental College, Los Angeles
Volume Author: Anita Dalal

for Brown Partworks
Project Editor: Lee Stacy
Designer: Sarah Williams
Picture Researcher: Helen Simm
Cartographer: Mark Walker
Indexer: Kay Ollerenshaw
Managing Editor: Tim Cooke
Design Manager: Lynne Ross
Production Manager: Matt Weyland

for Raintree Steck-Vaughn
Project Editor: Sean Dolan
Production Manager: Richard Johnson

Picture credits

Cover: Machu Picchu: N. J. Saunders; Tezcatlipoca mask: Werner Forman Archive/British Museum, London.

Ancient Art & Architecture Collection: 19, Israel Museum 21b, Ronald Sheridan 36b, James Sparshatt 20; **The Art Archive:** 31, National Anthropological Museum Mexico/Dagli Orti 24, Pedro de Osma Museum Lima/Mireille Vautier 17t, Nicolas Sapieha 39, Mireille Vautier 33t; **Bruce Coleman Collection:** Dr. Eckart Pott 15; **Corbis:** Charles & Josette Lenars 29b; **Rick Frehsee (Peabody Museum, Harvard University):** 27; **Image Bank:** Guido Albe Rossi 9t; **Mary Evans Picture Library:** 21t, 28, Explorer Archives 10b; **Peter Newark's American Pictures:** 25b, 37, 44; **N.J. Saunders:** 17b, 25t; **South American Pictures:** Tony Morrison 12, 13t, 16, 32, 33b, Chris Sharp 8, 23, 29t, 43; **Werner Forman Archive:** 41b, Biblioteca Universitaria Bologna 5, British Museum London 11, 35, Liverpool Museum 7, Museum Fur Volkerkunde Basel 36t, Museum Fur Volkerkunde Vienna 45, National Museum of Anthropology Mexico City 40, National Museum of Natural History Smithsonian Institution Washington 41t.

Contents

General Introduction

MYTHS ARE THE MIRRORS of humanity. They reflect the inner soul of a culture and try to give profound answers in a seemingly mysterious world. In other words, myths give the relevant culture an understanding of its place in the world and the universe in general. Found in all civilizations, myths sometimes combine fact and fiction and other times are complete fantasy. Regardless of their creative origin, myths are always dramatic.

Every culture has its own myths, yet globally there are common themes and symbols, even across civilizations that had no contact with or awareness of each other. Some of the most common types include those that deal with the creation of the world, the cosmos, or a particular site, like a large mountain or lake. Other myths deal with the origin of humans, or a specific people or civilization, or the heroes or gods who either made the world inhabitable or gave humans something essential, such as the ancient Greek Titan Prometheus, who gave fire, or the Ojibwa hero Wunzh, who was given divine instructions on cultivating corn. There are also myths about the end of the world, death and the afterlife, and the renewal or change of seasons.

The origin of evil and death are also common themes. Examples of such myths are the Biblical Eve eating the forbidden fruit or the ancient Greek story of Pandora opening the sealed box.

Additionally there are flood myths, myths about the sun and the moon, and myths of a peaceful, beautiful place of reward, such as heaven or Elysium, or of punishment, such as hell or Tartarus. Myths also teach important human values, such as courage. In all cases, myths show that the gods and their deeds are outside of ordinary human life and yet essential to it.

In this volume the most important myths of the pre-Columbian cultures of America are presented. Following each myth is an explanation of how the myth was either reflected in or linked to the real life of the particular civilization. There is also a glossary at the end of the volume to help identify the major mythological and historical characters, as well as explain many cultural terms.

PRE-COLUMBIAN MYTHOLOGY

Pre-Columbian cultures are those that originated in Mexico, Central America, and the Andes of South America before the Spanish conquered the New World in the 16th century. For thousands of years, highly advanced civilizations rose and fell in the area, leaving rich cultural and architectural legacies. The ancient Mixtecs, Olmecs, and Teotihuacans built large cities, made great agricultural advances, and practiced highly structured rituals related to sacred myths. These achievements and practices were adopted by later great empires, such as the Incas of the Andes and the Aztecs and Mayas of Mexico and Central America. Together these civilizations governed millions of people, but with the arrival of the Spanish they quickly crumbled.

As in many cultures, the myths of the pre-Columbian peoples reflected the conflicts and wonder of life and nature while justifying the aggressive, belligerent actions encouraged by their leaders. War was central to much of pre-Columbian life. To ensure the favor of the gods, some pre-Columbian civilizations, especially the Aztecs, practiced ritual human sacrifice.

But like our own, these sometimes violent cultures produced great achievements, such as expert astronomers and highly sophisticated and complex calendars, especially the Mayas and Aztecs. They developed their own hieroglyphics (picture words), architectural style, and wall paintings. Indeed, the Spanish conquerors of the Aztecs and Incas were astounded at the beauty and wealth of their capital cities. Also, sport, especially the sacred ball game *tlachtli*, was a central recreational and religious activity for many pre-Columbian civilizations.

Above: *Much of what we know of pre-Columbian mythology comes from picture texts called codices, like this one depicting the morning star (planet Venus) attacking jaguar warriors with spears.*

Creation of the Earth

The peoples of pre-Columbian America, like most ancient cultures, viewed their surroundings as both life sustaining and destructive. The theme of this Aztec creation myth is typical of the region: out of conflict comes good — in this case, nature.

AT THE BEGINNING of time there existed only the earth and the sky. The surface of the earth was covered in water, and the only types of creatures that dwelled there were the monsters. The sky was the home of the gods, who had a very unpredictable relationship with each other. Sometimes the gods worked together to defeat monsters or create worlds, other times they tried to destroy each other and all that existed.

One day in the sky two gods, Tezcatlipoca and Quetzalcoatl, were looking down on the earth when they happened to see a huge alligator-like monster swimming on the surface of the earth's water. In order to get a closer look the two gods flew down low. As they approached the creature, they saw that it was Tlaltecuhtli, a very greedy she-monster with an insatiable appetite. Tlaltecuhtli not only had a very large mouth full of sharp teeth in her face, but she had many other mouths all over her body, including on her feet and knees and running all the way up to her elbows and hands. Having so many mouths meant that Tlaltecuhtli could eat anything in or above the water.

Tezcatlipoca and Quetzalcoatl wanted to create dry land on the earth's surface, but they had to work out a way to stop Tlaltecuhtli from devouring it. The two gods turned themselves into two giant serpents and dove into the water to look for the hungry Tlaltecuhtli.

When they found her one of the serpent gods grabbed Tlaltecuhtli's left hand and right foot and the other serpent god took hold of the monster's right hand and left foot. Between them they started to pull harder and harder until the giant monster began to split in two. The lower half of Tlaltecuhtli's body rose up to form the heavens high above the sky, the top part of her body fell to form the solid land, and her spiny back became the earth's large mountains.

The other gods in the sky did not want dry land on earth. When they saw what Tezcatlipoca and Quetzalcoatl had done to Tlaltecuhtli, they became very angry. So to appease the other gods Tezcatlipoca and Quetzalcoatl quickly decided that they would use what was left of Tlaltecuhtli's body to make the rest of nature for living creatures to inhabit.

Above: *In another version of the myth, illustrated here in an Aztec codex, or book, from the 14th century, Tezcatlipoca tricked Tlaltecuhtli into swallowing his foot. The god's foot tore the monster apart, forming the earth's surface.*

From Tlaltecuhtli's hair the two gods made all the trees, flowers, and herbs, and from her skin, the grasses and flowers that cover the earth. The giant monster's eyes became the source of wells, springs, and small caves. Her many mouths were turned into great rivers and caverns that would later give shelter to humans and other creatures. Her nose was transformed into gentle hills and valleys. When Tezcatlipoca and Quetzalcoatl had finished their creation the other gods were very pleased with the result and forgave the two gods for transforming Tlaltecuhtli.

Major Pre-Columbian Cultures and Empires

The Mayas, Aztecs, and Incas developed rich and varied civilizations. Their achievements ranged from architectural and economic innovations to military and cultural conquests.

Below: *In Mayan society, an elongated forehead, as shown in this sculpture, was considered beautiful.*

By the early 16th century, when the Spanish conquistadores, led by adventurers like Hernando Cortés (1485–1547) and Francisco Pizarro (1475–1541), arrived in the so-called New World, they found many different civilizations. In the region known as Mesoamerica, which spread from central Mexico in the north to Nicaragua in the south and throughout the Andes of South America, there were three major cultures, the Mayas, the Aztecs, and the Incas.

Culturally, both the Mayas and Aztecs were influenced by much older Mesoamerican groups such as the Olmecs and Toltecs. Over several centuries the Olmecs, and later the Toltecs, developed cultures that excelled in art and architecture and had highly organized social structures.

The Olmecs, who lived in southern Mexico, were dominant between 1100 and 800 B.C. They developed architectural features, such as ball courts, pyramids, and city squares, as well as hieroglyphic writing (using pictures to signify words).

The Toltecs rose to power in A.D. 900 and controlled central Mexico for over 300 years. They were good architects and artists and left many sculptures showing their war victories against rivals such as the Mixtecs.

The Mayas, who lived in the Yucatán peninsula of present-day Mexico and Central America, developed a civilization that lasted from 1000 B.C. until the Spanish conquest in the early 16th century. Although they had no capital, the Mayas spread a common culture over a large area.

The Mayas were expert astronomers and mathematicians who invented their own hieroglyphic writing and produced codices (illustrated books), four of which still exist today. Each codex contains information about the Mayan religion. Together the codices describe the Mayan gods, many of which were the same gods worshiped by the Aztecs but with different names.

The Aztecs were originally a wandering tribe before they settled in the Valley of Mexico on swampy land where they founded the capital city of Tenochtitlán in around A.D. 1325. For two centuries the Aztecs dominated the area until their rule was ended by the Spanish in the 16th century.

A warring and aggressive society, the Aztecs demanded a tax in the form of labor from the people they conquered. But they also greatly respected the cultures of the people they conquered and often integrated the gods of those peoples into their own religion.

Their prime gods included Tlaloc, the god of rain, who may have been Olmec in origin, and Quetzalcoatl, who was often represented as a plumed serpent and was derived from Toltec mythology. On the other hand, Huitzilopochtli, the god of war, was an entirely Aztec creation and may have actually been an ancient Aztec leader.

SOUTH AMERICAN EMPIRE

From the early 15th century until the early 16th century the Incas controlled an empire that stretched along the Pacific coast from Ecuador in the north to central Chile in the south and included an estimated 12 million people. They had a capital city, Cuzco, founded in the 12th century, and ruled their vast empire by means of an efficient network of roads and bridges.

The Incas recorded information not by writing it down but by using a quipu. A quipu is a string with knots tied in different places and in different colors. Exactly how the Incas used it has yet to be deciphered.

Above: *Ancient Aztec clothing is still worn by modern-day Aztecs during celebrations held in Mexico.*

Left: *The famous Aztec capital of Tenochtitlán was built on Lake Texcoco and at its height spread some 5 square miles (8 sq. km).*

The Creation of Corn People

Agriculture – especially growing corn – was basic to the survival of pre-Columbian cultures. It was so important that this Mayan myth sees corn people as the ancestors of humans.

A T THE START OF THE WORLD people did not exist. In fact there were no animals of any kind. Nor was there any grass, flowers, or trees; only the sky, the oceans, the barren earth, and the gods.

Lying coiled at the bottom of the sea was the god Gucumatz, a plumed serpent. High in the sky was the god Huracan, also called Heart of Heaven, who appeared with bolts of lightning shooting from his head. Together the two gods discussed how they might create a world. As they were describing how it would look, mountains began to rise from the sea and forests covered the earth, just as they described.

The gods decided to put animals on the land. They asked the animals to pray and give thanks to their creators. But the animals could not speak. They could only squawk and make howling noises. So the gods decided to invent a creature that would rule over the animals and would praise the gods properly and feed them with prayers and offerings.

The creature they decided to make was a man. The first man was made from clay. He could speak, but only nonsense. His body was so weak that it started to crumble and dissolve. The gods broke him apart and started again. This time they made a man out of wood, and before they knew it the world was full of wooden men.

The wooden men could speak, but they were rude and lacked feelings. Worse still, they were not grateful to their creators and refused to pray to them. The wooden men were so mean that even their own cooking pots and animals turned against them. The gods decided to destroy them. They sent a huge flood to wash them away. The wooden men tried to escape the rising waters but failed.

After the flood the earth still had no creatures to rule over the animals. Seeking advice from other gods, Huracan and Gucumatz decided to make new men out of corn. They made four who were unlike any of the earlier men.

The corn men were highly intelligent and very grateful to their creators. But the gods were afraid that the corn men were too clever. So the gods decided to take away some of the corn men's wisdom and replace it with happiness in the form of four corn women. It is from the four corn men and four corn women that the whole of the human race is descended.

Left: *Found at an important Mayan city called Copán, this sculpture of a corn deity was made in A.D. 775. In an ancient ritual, a small amount of the Mayan ruler's blood was used to fertilize new crops of corn.*

Agriculture in Pre-Columbian America

In pre-Columbian society the most common occupation was that of farmer. But the way pre-Columbian farmers toiled the land varied from region to region, depending on the nature of their surroundings, from rain forest to floating gardens.

Most early Mesoamericans lived in small villages where they grew corn, beans, squashes, chili peppers, and cotton. Of these different kinds of crop, corn proved the most dependable and versatile. As the mighty Mesoamerican civilizations — beginning with the Olmecs in the 11th century B.C. to the Aztecs and Mayas in the early 16th century — grew and expanded, corn remained the main crop.

To store harvested corn Mesoamericans mixed ripe kernels with water and white lime to make a preservative. This process was known as *mixtamal*, and it enabled corn to be stored and later ground for many different types of dishes, including tamales and tortillas, year round.

Although the warm climate of south Mexico and Central America made growing corn easy, there were some problems. The crop could only be farmed for a few years on the same patch of land before it depleted the soil's nutrients. To prevent this, Mesoamerican farmers, like today's farmers, practiced crop rotation and planted secondary crops, such as beans and squashes, along with corn, which would replenish the soil.

Below: *Farmers in the Andes have continued the ancient Inca practice of terrace farming.*

In addition, Mayan farmers had the problem of having to carve out farm land from the Yucatán's tropical rain forest. To make the most of this environment, they practiced slash-and-burn farming, still used today by their Mayan descendants.

They cut down forest, burned the trees, and planted seed on the cleared land. The soil in the exposed land was usually of poor quality, and only two to four years of farming was possible. For those Mayas who lived at higher elevations, the land was of better quality and could be farmed for about 10 years.

INCA TERRACE FARMING

For farmers in South America methods of farming were very different from those used in Mesoamerica. For instance, some of the inhabitants of the enormous Inca empire lived on the steep slopes of the Andes Mountains. In these high-altitude areas the potato, not corn, was the primary crop.

Above: *To clear forests for farming land, the ancient Mayas would cut down and burn trees and vegetation. Their descendants continue this slash-and-burn method of agriculture.*

To make the mountainous terrain suitable for cultivation, Inca farmers practiced terrace farming by cutting out level terraces that appear like giant steps running up the side of a mountain. The terraces retained water and prevented fertile soil from washing away. The descendants of the Inca continue to practice terrace farming, although on a smaller scale than their ancestors.

Floating Gardens

The Aztecs' method of farming was unusual in Mesoamerica. They farmed on floating gardens. In a unique feat of engineering, the Aztecs reclaimed the swamp land (on Lake Texcoco) on which their capital, Tenochtitlán, was founded, and placed flat reeds on top of marshland. They then covered the platforms with soil on which they farmed. These "floating gardens" produced large crops, and at the height of the Aztec's power as many as 300,000 people left the city each morning in small boats to tend their floating gardens.

Coniraya Viracocha

The spirit Coniraya Viracocha was at times mischievous. He even pretended to be the mighty Viracocha, who the Incas believed was the force behind all creation.

AT A TIME NOT LONG after the creation of people, the earth was still populated by nature spirits. There were also animals, but they had not yet been given all their characteristics. It was during this era that the spirit Coniraya Viracocha decided to wander the earth disguised as a beggar to interact with people.

One day a beautiful woman, Cavillaca, sat weaving beneath a tree. She had many admirers but lived alone. Passing by, Coniraya Viracocha saw her and immediately fell in love. He turned himself into a bird and flew into the tree to be near her. Cavillaca loved the tree's fruit and ate some of it. When she ate the fruit that Coniraya had touched, it made her pregnant.

The child Cavillaca bore was a boy, and on his first birthday she summoned all the men of her village to find out who the father was. The men came dressed in their best clothes, but no one admitted to being the father. Cavillaca decided to put the baby on the floor and see who he would crawl to.

Coniraya, dressed only in rags, tried to hide quietly in a corner, but the baby crawled straight to him. Cavillaca was furious when she realized that a scruffy beggar was the father of her baby. In her anger she took her baby and fled.

When Coniraya heard that Cavillaca had left he rushed after her. On his way he met a condor, who told the spirit that he would soon catch Cavillaca. To show his thanks Coniraya blessed the condor with the power to fly above mountains and to nest where it would be safe.

Next Coniraya met a fox, who said Cavillaca was so far away that he would never catch her. Angry with the fox's words, Coniraya cursed the animal so that it would always be unloved.

Finally, he met some macaws, who told him he was too late. Cavillaca and her baby had turned into rocks the moment they reached the sea. Although this was the truth, Coniraya cursed the macaws by making them sing so loud that they would always be heard by their predators.

When Coniraya finally got to the coast he found the rocks that had once been Cavillaca and her baby. He was so angry that he tipped the fish from a local goddess's pond into the sea. From these fish come all the fish in the sea. The goddess was furious and tried to kill Coniraya, but the crafty spirit managed to escape.

Above: *According to the myth of Coniraya Viracocha, the beautiful Cavillaca and her young son were turned into rocks when they reached the seashore. The myth also provides an explanation for other aspects of nature, such as the loud noise made by macaws, the birds that witnessed Cavillaca's transformation.*

The Hierarchical Nature of Inca Society

At its height the Inca empire was the largest in South America, governing an estimated 12 million people. The rulers were only able to maintain order due to a firmly structured society.

Inca society was very inflexible. Whatever social position a person was born into was the one in which he or she remained. This goes some way toward explaining why the people in the myth did not recognize the spirit Coniraya Viracocha when he was dressed in old rags — spirits were supposed to wear finer clothes.

At the top of Inca society was the ruler of the empire, who called himself the Inca. He was considered to be a direct descendant of the creator being known as Viracocha, a deity adopted from pre-Inca civilizations. The Inca ruler was also thought to be the human representative of Viracocha, thus making his position and power absolute. Directly below the Inca ruler was the royal family, which was made up of the Inca's wives, girlfriends, and their many children.

Next in order of importance were the priests and nobles. Together, these top layers of the society made up the

Below: *The Incas were extremely fine craftspeople. This ancient silver llama is typical of the kind of treasures the Spanish sent home to Spain.*

aristocracy. The ordinary members of the Inca empire were at the bottom of the hierarchy.

Every member of Inca society belonged to an *ayllu*, or social group, to which they were loyal. The *ayllus* formed the basis of Inca government and allowed the Incas to rule over a very large geographical area.

The imperial administration and religious posts were filled by high-ranking noblemen and priests from the royal *ayllu*. Working for them were the regional *ayllu* chiefs, whose job it was to organize the payment of *mita* and to maintain peace and order across an empire of about 12 million people.

PAYING INCA TAX

Mita was a kind of tax that was paid in the form of goods such as weapons, cloth, wool, potatoes, and corn. The way *mita* worked was that every ordinary member of the Inca empire, excluding the aristocracy, was expected to divide his land and goods into three parts. One third of the land was given to the emperor and state, another third to the priests, gods, and sun, and the final third to the person's local *ayllu*. By dividing land and goods three ways, the emperor was able to increase his own wealth and keep in check his conquered people, who were left with nothing for themselves.

Right: *Viracocha Inca, ruler of the Incas in the early 15th century, began the expansion of the empire by conquering and taking the lands of neighboring tribes.*

Below: *The city of Machu Picchu lies in the Andes a few miles from Cuzco. It was found by the explorer Hiram Bingham in 1911.*

In addition, every province in the empire had to pay a set amount to the imperial capital, Cuzco. This other type of tax was based on the number of people living in the community.

During the 15th century, as a result of the absolute power of the ruler Viracocha Inca and the system of *mita*, Inca society was more structured than any other society in the world at that time. Since everyone belonged to an *ayllu* their individual behavior was considered to affect not only their social group but all those in *ayllus* above them in the social order.

The *ayllu* was such a dominant part of people's lives that the notion of individual freedom did not exist. This lack of personal freedom left many within the Inca empire unhappy. Historians reached this conclusion in part because the language of Indian peasants who lived in the countryside contains many words to describe the feeling of unhappiness.

The Origin of Cuzco

About 15 miles (24 km) outside of Cuzco, the ancient Inca capital, is Mt. Paqaritampu. Along the mountain's cliff face lie three small caves, and it is from the middle cave that the Incas believed the founders of their royal dynasty emerged.

ONE DAY, MANY CENTURIES AGO, four brothers and their four sisters came out of a cave on Paqaritampu. The siblings dressed very differently from the local people who lived alongside the mountain. The creator god Viracocha had told the siblings to set off on foot and look for a site on which to build a city.

As they climbed the mountains that surround Paqaritampu, the eldest brother, Ayar Cachi, whose name means "salt," started to show off. At the top of a mountain called Huanacauri, in a village of the same name, Ayar Cachi got out his sling and started to hurl stones. He was so strong that as the stones hit the neighboring hills their force caused ravines to appear. His brothers were extremely angry with Ayar Cachi for showing off and so devised a plan to punish him.

They persuaded him to return to the cave, and when he stepped inside they quickly walled up the entrance, trapping Ayar Cachi inside. The others then carried on their journey, but the second brother, Ayar Ucho, whose name means "pepper," decided to stay in the village of Huanacauri. He turned himself into stone so that he might become immortal and be worshiped as a shrine. The third brother, Ayar Sauca, whose name means "joy," also decided that he did not want to continue the search for a site for the new city. Instead, he chose to live with the peasants and become a spirit of the fields.

This left only one brother, Ayar Manco, and his four sisters. Together they continued on their quest until they reached a spot miles from where they had started. Mama Ocllo, one of the sisters, said, "Let's build our capital city here." Using a gold stick they had brought with them on the journey, they tapped the ground to discover where the exact center of the city should be. Then Ayar Manco, who from then on was known as Manco Capac, married his sister, Mama Ocllo. Together they became the first Inca rulers.

They set about building the beautiful city, which they called Cuzco, intending that it should reflect the glory of Viracocha. In his honor they constructed a temple and built many magnificent buildings and palaces. Manco Capac, Mama Ocllo, and the nobles of the Inca empire would live in Cuzco for many years.

Above: *Manco Capac was the first ruler of the Incas and founder of the Inca capital, Cuzco. This illustration of the Inca ruler dates from sometime during the early 16th century, when the Spanish conquered the Incas and began building on top of Cuzco's original sites.*

Grand City of the Incas

The capital of the Inca empire, Cuzco was a splendid city built with amazing engineering. Little of the original city remains, however, having been built over by the Spanish.

Manco Capac and Mama Ocllo were actually real people who founded Cuzco and the Inca royal dynasty in the 12th century A.D. During the reign of a later Inca ruler, Pachacuti, in the 15th century, the Incas expanded their territory by conquering neighboring cultures. It was during this period that Cuzco, which remains a city in southern Peru, became the grand center of the Inca empire. Pachacuti himself oversaw the redevelopment of the capital.

Cuzco, which means "navel" or "center" in the Quechua language, lies in a valley at a height of 11,500 feet (3,500 m). Pachacuti turned two local rivers into canals and built a ceremonial square over one of them at the center of the city.

The city was planned to resemble the shape of a puma, because the Incas considered the big cat a symbol of strength. A fortress that protected the center was located at the puma's head, and at the puma's tail the two canals

Above: *An Inca stone wall, one of the few remaining examples of Inca architecture. The Spanish destroyed or built over most Inca buildings.*

Left: *The Inca empire during the 15th and early 16th centuries.*

Right: *Inca Pachacuti greatly expanded the empire in the 15th century.*

merged. Within the animal shape the city was arranged in a grid, with the narrow paved streets crossing at right angles, just like many modern American cities. The central part was also divided into four sections to represent the four corners of the empire.

REBUILDING THE CAPITAL

It took 50,000 builders and craftsmen 20 years to create the imperial city. The streets had stone gutters for water and sewage drainage, and the buildings were made out of hard volcanic rock that workmen carefully cut into large blocks and then fitted tightly together without mortar. The blocks interlocked so exactly that even today it is impossible to slip a piece of paper between them.

Below: *This pair of wooden Inca keros (cups) were made around the time of the Spanish conquest of the Inca empire in the early 16th century.*

The heart of ancient Cuzco was the ceremonial square, which was about the same size and position of the present-day Plaza de Armas. Four main streets led off the square, one to each corner of the empire. People resided in the district that matched their place of origin, so somebody from the eastern part of the empire would live in the eastern district.

Only the Inca (ruler), like Pachacuti, high-ranking nobles, and conquered chieftains could live in the heart of the capital. The lower a person's social rank, the farther away he lived from the center.

Within Cuzco stood the most sacred place in the Inca empire, the Temple of the Sun. Worshipers traveled from the four corners of the empire to visit it. Today, a curved wall of the temple survives intact, although the Spanish built the Santo Domingo church on top of the Inca temple.

The Ball Game in the Underworld

The ball game tlachtli *was popular across Mesoamerica. For the Mayas the ball game was so important that two of their most revered mythological characters were expert players.*

THE TWIN BROTHERS Hunhun-Ahpu and Vukub-Ahpu loved playing the ball game *tlachtli* and practiced hard until they were the best players in the world. The lords of the underworld kingdom of Xibalba were also good players and grew jealous of the twins' talent, eventually challenging them to a game.

When they descended into Xibalba the twins found that they had been tricked. They would first have to overcome a series of obstacles before even reaching the ball court. The brothers failed at the obstacles, and the evil lords demanded their death. The twins bravely agreed and were put to death.

Their bodies were buried, but the head of Hunhun-Ahpu was hung in a tree in Xibalba as a trophy. Until that day the tree had never borne any fruit, but immediately its branches were full. The lords then forbid the touching of the tree.

One day, a curious young girl named Xquiq could not resist plucking one of the fruit. As she stretched out her hand the head of Hunhun-Ahpu spat on her palm. "Quick," the head told her, "hurry to the upperworld where you will bear my sons." The girl was scared but fled Xibalba with the evil lords in hot pursuit.

Having reached the upperworld, Xquiq gave birth to twin sons, whom she named Hunahpu and Xbalanque. The twins grew into strong and clever men who also became players of *tlachtli*.

The lords challenged Hunahpu and Xbalanque to a game of *tlachtli*, and the twins descended into Xibalba, just as their father and uncle had done years earlier. Unlike their father, however, the twins knew that the lords would try to trick them. They overcame the challenges, and when they finally got to play the ball game they defeated the lords.

After the game the evil lords forced the twins to go through another series of challenges, but this time the clever brothers set a trap of their own. They pretended to be defeated and allowed the lords to burn them on a funeral pyre. Their ashes were scattered but five days later two strange figures — half-men, half-fish — appeared. The new creatures performed tricks, burning down and then remaking animals.

The lords of Xibalba were impressed and asked the strange figures to burn them as well. As the lords disappeared into the flames the brothers threw off their disguises and shouted that the evil lords would not be re-created.

Left: *This modern statue of an ancient Mayan* tlachtli *ball player stands in Guatemala, which was once part of the Mayan empire.*

23

The Sacred Ball Game

Each Mesoamerican group had its own variation of tlachtli and treated the winners and losers differently. Some groups sacrificed the winners, others the losers.

Throughout all cultures in ancient Mesoamerica, wherever there was a religious temple there was also usually a sacred ball court nearby. The ball court was used to play the game known as *tlachtli*.

Although some historians and archaeologists believe that the game originated with the ancient Olmecs, no one knows for sure who actually invented it or how old *tlachtli* really is. However, all experts on pre-Columbian America agree that the ball game was an important part of Mayan and other Mesoamerican cultures, as the myth of Hunahpu and Xbalanque shows.

In some ways the ball game was an early ancestor of modern basketball and soccer. A typical court was shaped like the capital letter "I" and was oriented either east to west or north to south. The court was usually enclosed by high stone walls on which were carved sculptures of the gods and demons to whom the game was dedicated.

The object of the game was to get a solid rubber ball through one of two stone hoops placed opposite each other high on the court walls. The difficulty was that the players of the two opposing teams could not use their feet or hands. Instead they had to use their elbows, knees, or hips, which were all protected with heavy padding.

RELIGIOUS MEANING

Some archaeologists believe that for several Mesoamerican cultures the court represented heaven and the ball either the sun, moon, or stars. The rings through which the ball was hit symbolized either the sunrise or sunset, or perhaps even the fall and spring equinoxes (when daytime and nighttime are of equal length).

Others theorize that the whole game symbolized an effort to control fate. This interpretation claims that the ball represented fate, which was at the

Below: Ball court markers, such as the one shown here, which dates from around A.D. 650, were used to divide the court between the two teams.

Left: *The "I" shape design of the ancient* tlachtli *ball court at El Tajín was common across most of Mesoamerica.*

Below: *To score in* tlachtli *the ball had to be shot through the hole in the hoop high above the court floor. This illustrated reconstruction shows players at the grand ball court at Chichén Itzá.*

mercy of the players, and the result of the game was always uncertain.

In keeping with the religious importance of the game, it is believed that the captain of the winning team in Mayan society was sacrificed to the gods. In Aztec society, however, it is thought that the losing player was sacrificed, so that his life would give birth to the new sun.

Historians also believe that in Aztec society only the nobles were allowed to play the ball game. But at the same time the sport, which was usually played during religious festivals, was enjoyed by spectators. They would place bets on the outcome.

The Grand Ball Court at Chichén Itzá

The ball court at the Mayan city of Chichén Itzá, which was controlled by the Toltecs from the 10th to late 12th centuries, is the largest and grandest ever found in Mesoamerica. At both long ends of the ball court lie two small temples, with the one at the north end housing many fine stone reliefs depicting Toltec culture. On top of the east wall of the ball court is another temple that has frescoes of the Toltec invasion of the Mayan territories in the Yucatán.

Vucub Caquix Battles the Twins

The heavenly twins feature in several important Mayan myths that appear in the Popol Vuh, a famous book of Mayan mythology written in the 16th century.

Before the creation of humans, there lived a boastful bird god called Vucub Caquix who pretended he was the sun, moon, and light. Offended by the bird god's arrogance, the heavenly twins, Hunahpu and Xbalanque, waged a war against the impostor in order to destroy him.

The heavenly twins knew that Vucub Caquix liked to eat the fruit of a particular tree, so they waited nearby for the bird god to turn up. When he appeared for his daily meal the twins fired arrows, wounding the impostor. But the bird god did not give up easily and fought with the heavenly twins. Vucub Caquix pulled off one of Hunahpu's arms and made off with it.

To retrieve the arm the twins got a crafty old man and his wife to help. The old couple went in search of Vucub Caquix and found him suffering from both a toothache and sore eyes. Knowing that his powerful strength came from his teeth and that he needed his vision, they convinced him that they could heal his ailments.

First, the crafty old couple pulled out all the bird god's teeth and replaced them with sharp grains of corn. Then they promptly gorged out

the bird god's eyes. Vucub Caquix had now lost all his power and sight, and he could not stop the crafty old couple from seizing Hunahpu's severed arm. When the old couple took the severed arm to Hunahpu, the heavenly twin easily fixed it back in place.

But the battle was not yet over. Vucub Caquix had two sons — Zipacna and Cabraca — who were determined to carry on their father's fight against the heavenly twins. Zipacna's other name was "creator of mountains" because at night he carried the mountains on his back. During the day he hunted for fresh fish and crabs.

One day, Zipacna came across 400 warriors who were trying to carry a giant log to prop up the roof of their enormous house. He offered to help and was so strong that he carried the giant log all on his own. But the warriors were allies of the heavenly twins. Recognizing Zipacna, they devised a plan to destroy him.

After he had delivered the giant log they coaxed Zipacna into a deep pit and buried him. Zipacna realized that it was a trap but played along by pretending to be dead. Believing they had killed him, the warriors returned to their

Above: *A sculpture of Vucub Caquix, the bird god, can be found at the Mayan ball court in Copán. The original, which dates from around A.D. 450, has been reconstructed in plaster, shown here. The severed arm of the heavenly twin Hunahpu lies in the mouth of the serpent's head that comes out from the center of the bird god.*

house to celebrate. Zipacna then quietly snuck up to the warriors' house and pulled it down, killing them all. In their death the warriors turned into stars.

To avenge the warriors' deaths, the heavenly twins made a model of a large and very tasty crab. They used the fake crab to lure Zipacna to a cave inside a mountain. When he was about to eat the crab the mountain fell on top of him.

Next the twins turned their attention to Zipacna's brother, Cabraca. The twins took him hunting and fed him the birds they had caught. Cabraca did not know that the heavenly twins had basted the birds with deadly poisonous earth. Cabraca died after only a few bites.

With the defeat of Vucub Caquix and his two sons the world was finally safe enough for the heavenly twins to create humans.

Mayan Life and Myths in Pictures

The Mayas painted their mythological characters on walls and ceramics, and told of their exploits in texts known as codices, using picture-words called hieroglyphics.

The story of Hunahpu and Xbalanque's fight with Vucub Caquix can be found in the sacred Mayan book, the *Popol Vuh*. The *Popol Vuh*, which dates from the mid–16th century, was written by Mayan scribes in their own language but used Spanish letters. The stories tell of the battles of the gods and their attempts to create a creature — man — that would be able to worship its creator.

The *Popol Vuh* is an excellent source for anyone who wants to learn more about the Mayas. Another essential source for researchers is a series of texts known as the codices. Only four Mayan codices exist, and three are named for the European cities where they are kept — Dresden, Madrid, and Paris. While the Dresden Codex is considered the finest and most complete, the Grolier Codex, which is

Below: *The Mayas painted representations of their gods on this ancient vase.*

the fourth and is held privately, is the oldest. It dates from A.D. 1230 and is the one most recently discovered by archaeologists, in 1971.

DECIPHERING A CULTURE

The codices were made out of folded strips of bark covered with gypsum gesso (made with glue and used for painting on). The writers used pens made from feathers that they dipped in red or black paint. With the pens they drew symbols that together form a story. The translation of the symbols greatly increased historians' knowledge of Mayan culture.

Above: *The codex held in Dresden is a prime source for researchers studying Mayan culture.*

Right: *Bonampak, covered in growth today, was a main Mayan site some 1,400 years ago.*

Below: *Map of the Mayan civilization at its height.*

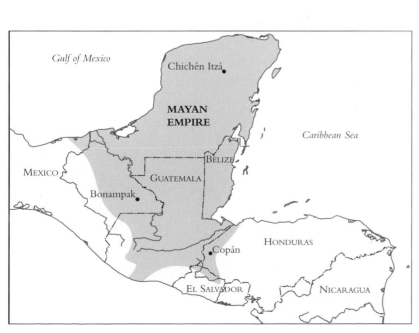

That knowledge continues to grow as archaeologists discover new sites and learn to decipher the symbols carved into the sides of buildings. Many Mayan sites were built in dense jungle, and over the centuries trees and vegetation have overgrown the structures. As these sites are uncovered they reveal more about how the Mayas really lived.

Mayan mythology appears on many carvings on the sides of temples. For

example, at Chichén Itzá's Temple of Jaguars, the adventures of the heavenly twins are recorded on the wall of the sacred ball court. At the ball court at Copán, a site in present-day Honduras, Vucub Caquix appears as a macaw.

One of the most exciting discoveries of Mayan sites was Bonampak in the forest of the southern Mexican state of Chiapas. There, murals dating from before A.D. 800 were found that tell, in great colorful detail, the story of a victorious Mayan battle and the victory celebrations that followed.

The Birth of Huitzilopochtli

The battle between Huitzilopochtli and Coyolxauhqui is a myth of conflict, a common theme throughout the mythologies of Mesoamerica. Such conflicts came from observing nature, which can be both nurturing and destructive.

THE GODDESS COATLICUE, also known as the Lady of the Serpent Skirt, was the mother of the Aztec gods. One day when she was sweeping out the temple at Coatepec, which was a sacred mountain close to the ancient Toltec city of Tula, a ball of feathers floated down to the ground. They were very beautiful and Coatlicue picked them up. She tucked them into her waistband so that she could take them away with her. Later, when she got home and looked for the ball of feathers, it had disappeared. Unknown to Coatlicue the feathers had special powers and they had made her pregnant with the mighty Huitzilopochtli, god of war and sacrifice.

Coatlicue had already given birth to many gods, and as her womb grew larger her sons wanted to know who the father of her unborn child was. When she could not give them a name they told their warrior sister, Coyolxauhqui.

Coyolxauhqui was the leader of all her brothers and a strong and fearless fighter. She was very angry with their mother for getting pregnant without her permission and made sure

that her brothers viewed their mother and the unborn child as enemies. She also convinced them that the only way to deal with the situation was to kill Coatlicue before she gave birth.

When Coatlicue found out what her children were planning she was very frightened. But the child growing in her womb told her not to worry, saying, "Have no fear, already I know what I must do."

Soon afterward Coyolxauhqui and her brothers followed Coatlicue to the mountain of Coatepec, where they planned to kill her. The young gods rushed up the mountain in full battle dress, screaming their war cries. Just as they reached the top of the mountain and were ready to attack, Coatlicue gave birth to Huitzilopochtli. He emerged from his mother's belly fully grown and dressed as an armed warrior. In his hand was a burning weapon, a serpent of fire, known as Xiuhcoatl, or Turquoise Serpent.

Brandishing his burning weapon, the newborn Huitzilopochtli faced his warrior sister Coyolxauhqui in battle and with one strong

Above: *This 16th-century drawing of Huitzilopochtli brandishing his serpent of fire was made by Bernardino de Sahagún, one of the first Spanish priests to arrive in Mesoamerica.*

swipe cut off her head. He then quickly sliced her body into a hundred tiny pieces that tumbled down the mountainside.

When the other brothers saw what the mighty Huitzilopochtli had done to their warrior sister they started to flee. But Huitzilopochtli was so fast and angry that he chased his half-brothers around the mountain until he caught them. Huitzilopochtli killed many of them so that they could not harm Coatlicue. However, he let a few of his half-brothers escape to the south, after which they were never seen again.

Huitzilopochtli's Temple

Tenochtitlán was a remarkable city built almost entirely on top of Lake Texcoco. It was also the most densely populated city in Mesoamerica, with an estimated 400,000 inhabitants.

In 1978 an electrical company digging in Mexico City made an exciting archaeological discovery. In the heart of the city they uncovered the ancient Aztec capital, Tenochtitlán, and the remains of the Great Pyramid, which was dedicated to the most important Aztec deity, Huitzilopochtli.

The only god to belong exclusively to the Aztecs — most of their gods were adopted from cultures they had dominated — Huitzilopochtli, it was told, led the Aztecs to the site of their new city. There they found an eagle sitting on a cactus with a serpent in its beak. The eagle told the Aztecs that this was where they were to build Tenochtitlán, their capital.

At the heart of the city was the Great Pyramid dedicated to Huitzilopochtli. It was used for every kind of ceremonial event, including human sacrifice. One of the most important rituals, which involved different stages, was the inauguration of a new king.

On the death of a ruler, the heir to the throne withdrew from society. Dressed only in a loincloth he was led by two noblemen to the bottom of the Great Pyramid. As a sign of humility the ruler-to-be was supported up the pyramid stairs by the noblemen to Huitzilopochtli's shrine.

There he was dressed in a dark green cape with skull and crossbones designs on it, representing his withdrawal from the present and a return to the dawn of time. Incense was burned in front of

Left: *This recent excavation site in Mexico City shows the remains of the Great Pyramid of Tenochtitlán, which was dedicated to the Aztec god Huitzilopochtli.*

Left: *This 16th-century illustration shows the moment when the ancient Aztecs, guided by their god Huitzilopochtli, found the eagle with a serpent in its mouth, indicating that this was where they should build Tenochtitlán.*

the shrine before the new ruler went down the stairs. The mood was very somber among the watching crowd.

Four days of fasting followed for the new ruler, during which time he contemplated his new godlike role and carried out religious purification ceremonies. Meanwhile, a silent procession visited Huitzilopochtli's shrine each noon and midnight to burn incense.

CROWNING THE NEW KING

The coronation was a big contrast to the somber mood of the retreat. To assume his new position and mark his return to society the ruler went to one of the royal palaces where he was dressed in the robes of state.

A crown of gold and green stones was placed on his head, and emeralds pierced his nose and ears. On his arms and ankles were gold bracelets and on his feet jaguar-skin sandals. Once dressed, the new king sat on a throne decorated with eagle feathers and jaguar hides.

Finally, the king was carried on his throne to the top of the Great Pyramid to Huitzilopochtli's shrine, where he used a jaguar's claw to cut his skin and release some blood. Once he offered his blood, more prayers and sermons followed and an offering of quail was made to cement the bond between the new ruler and Huitzilopochtli.

Left: *Archaeologists believe that these Aztec stone figures, found at the foot of the Great Pyramid of Tenochtitlán, were carved in A.D. 1413.*

Tezcatlipoca's Revenge

In Aztec mythology the relationship between gods could change. Although they had worked together to create the earth (see page 6), Tezcatlipoca and Quetzalcoatl were also enemies.

THE GOD QUETZALCOATL was very clever and very kind. He knew many things, such as where corn was hidden, the value of precious metals such as gold and silver, and the use of different plants. All this information he passed on to the Toltecs.

All the Toltec people loved Quetzalcoatl, but the god Tezcatlipoca was very angry because Quetzalcoatl was so popular. Tezcatlipoca was the opposite of Quetzalcoatl. He was unpredictable, but because he had given man life he expected sacrifices from the Toltecs.

One day Tezcatlipoca visited Quetzalcoatl and held up a mirror. Quetzalcoatl saw his reflection and was upset that he had become a wrinkled old man with sunken eyes. Worried that his people would turn against him, Quetzalcoatl covered his face and ran away. Tezcatlipoca followed him and persuaded him to look in the mirror again. This time Quetzalcoatl saw a handsome man. Happy, Quetzalcoatl went back to his palace.

Tezcatlipoca, however, was not satisfied with just showing off his magical powers to Quetzalcoatl. He wanted to destroy him. The jealous god decided to pretend to be Quetzalcoatl's friend.

He offered him a special drink of *pulque*, a liquor made from the sap of the agave plant. At first Quetzalcoatl refused to taste the drink, but Tezcatlipoca would not give up and kept offering it to him. Finally, Quetzalcoatl took a sip, and liking the taste, another and then another. Soon he was drunk. He asked his sister, Quetzalpetlatl, to drink with him and soon she too was drunk.

For a while Quetzalcoatl and his sister lived a life of pleasure. They spent their days partying and forgot all about their religious duties. Then one day when they were not as drunk as usual they realized how irresponsible they had been.

Quetzalcoatl was overcome with guilt. He ordered a stone coffin made, and for four days he lay in the coffin as a penance. Then, on the fifth day, he went to the sea, followed by his people. There, they built a funeral pyre and Quetzalcoatl dressed in his finest clothes. He threw himself into the flames. The fire burned all day and night and Quetzalcoatl's body turned into ashes. There was nothing anybody could do, and as they watched helplessly they noticed a new star burning very brightly in the sky. Quetzalcoatl had become the morning star.

Above: *The Aztec god Tezcatlipoca was associated with the idea of destiny. Since death is inevitable, one representation of the god was this mask made of turquoise and lignite mosaic set over a human skull.*

Battling Gods and Sacrifice

Ritual sacrifice was common in Meso-america, but the Aztecs took the practice to extremes, sometimes conducting a series of human sacrifices lasting several days.

When the Aztecs conquered another culture or group they often adopted the gods of that culture as their own. The best example of this is the Toltec god Quetzalcoatl. The Aztecs considered the Toltecs the most noble of all the different civilizations and made Quetzalcoatl one of their most revered gods. Only Huitzilopochtli, the only original Aztec god, could rival Quetzalcoatl's popularity. Many of the Aztec myths are about Quetzalcoatl and his relationship with other Aztec gods, particularly Tezcatlipoca.

Sometimes, as in the myth, Quetzal-coatl and Tezcatlipoca fought against each other, and at other times they worked together, such as when they created the world out of the alligator-like monster Tlaltecuhtli. The changing nature of the two gods relation-ship represented the unpredictability of life.

They thought that the only way to try to maintain order in the world — that is, to guarantee that the sun rose every day and that the crops would grow — was through a combination of warfare and human sacrifice.

SCHEDULING WARFARE

Wars became a regular event of Aztec life and even started on set dates. Between 1450 and 1519 there was a series of wars, known as the Wars of the Flowers, in which the Aztecs fought a number of organized battles with warriors from kingdoms to the east of the empire. But the Aztecs fought wars

Above: *During the Aztec farming festival a warrior wore the skin of a person recently sacrificed. Similarly, this statue of Xipe Totec, god of vegetation, was made to appear to be dressed in human skin symbolizing the dry husk covering a growing seed.*

Left: *Sacrificial knives, like this eagle warrior stone blade from about A.D. 1400, were finely decorated.*

not just to expand their empire but also to maintain a steady supply of victims for human sacrifice. They believed that the braver a captive was, the more nourishing he would be for the gods.

Prisoners of war were not the only ones to be sacrificed. Occasionally women and even Aztec warriors were fed to the gods. Indeed, Aztec soldiers believed that the two most honorable deaths were on the battlefield and as a human sacrifice. It was to Huitzilopochtli, god of war and sacrifice, to whom most sacrifices were made.

Aztec sacrifice reflected a general religious belief in Mesoamerica. It was based on the idea that the gods had willingly made sacrifices to create the world and humans, and it was, therefore, the responsibility of everyone on earth to repay the gods' sacrifice through their own human sacrifice. In addition, Mesoamericans believed that the gods, although supernatural, were mortal and so needed food to stay alive. The Mayas thought that ritual bloodletting was a good way of feeding the gods, because human blood was the best food that the gods could possibly eat.

Below: *Prisoners of war were often sacrificed by the Aztecs. This 16th-century illustration shows the Aztecs leading warrior victims to sacrifice.*

Aztec Ritual Sacrifice

· ·

There were many different levels of sacrifice carried out at the Great Pyramid in Tenochtitlán, from the sacrifice of a slave to a minor god to spectacular ceremonies during which hundreds or thousands of captives were sacrificed. The Aztecs believed that the best food for the gods was a freshly beating heart, and the sacrificial ceremonies always followed the same procedure. The sacrificial stone where the victims were killed was at the top of a steep flight of steps of the pyramid. The victim had to climb the steps where four priests awaited him. Then he was laid out by the priests across the stone and his heart was cut out of his chest by an official. The heart was then burned and offered to the gods while the corpse was pushed down the steps. If the victim had been a brave soldier or a nobleman his corpse was carried down the stairs.

The Five Suns

The Aztecs believed there were four worlds, each with its own ruling sun, that preceded the current one. Each of the previous suns and worlds were dramatically destroyed by dueling gods.

IN THE BEGINNING the Creator Couple, Tonacatecuhtli and Tonacacihuatl, gave birth to sons who out of jealousy battled with each other to create the heavens, the earth, the sea, the underworld, and fire. The sons also made the first humans and the sacred calendar.

Tezcatlipoca, one of the sons, ruled over the first world, which was known as the Sun of the Earth. Giants roamed this world who were so strong they could pull up trees with their bare hands. Quetzalcoatl, Tezcatlipoca's brother, punched him into the sea to get rid of him. But Tezcatlipoca rose out of the ocean and turned himself into a giant jaguar. When he returned to earth he brought many jaguars that ate the giants.

Another new world was created, known as the Sun of the Wind, with Quetzalcoatl as its ruler. Tezcatlipoca, who was still angry with Quetzalcoatl, hit him causing a huge wind. As a result, Quetzalcoatl and all his creatures were carried off by the strong winds. The ones left became monkeys and swung high in the trees.

The third world, called the Sun of Rain, was ruled by Tlaloc, another son of the Creator Couple. But Quetzalcoatl destroyed the third world with fiery rain that poured down on all of Tlaloc's creatures turning them into turkeys.

The fourth world was the Sun of Water and Tlaloc's wife, Chalchiuhtlicue, ruled over it. This time Tezcatlipoca sent a great flood that was so big it washed away mountains, causing the heavens to crash into the fourth world. At the same time all of Chalchiuhtlicue's creatures were turned into fish.

Following the end of the fourth world the gods joined together and decided that the fifth world should be created by one of the gods sacrificing himself in a bonfire. The first god to volunteer for the sacrifice was a very proud and rich god called Tecuciztecatl. But the other gods wanted to sacrifice Nanahuatzin, a very poor and sick god whose body was covered in sores. As the gods built up the fire, Tecuciztecatl made offerings of precious jewelry. All that Nanahuatzin had to offer were some fir branches and balls of grass.

After four days of preparations the gods dressed for the fiery sacrifice. Tecuciztecatl wore fine clothes, but Nanahuatzin's costume was made out of paper. The rich god ran toward the fire and stopped as he felt the heat. Three more times he tried to jump in and failed.

Then it was Nanahuatzin's turn. The poor god jumped into the flames at the first try and became the fifth sun, known as Nahui Ollin, which shone brightly over the new earth. Tecuciztecatl was so ashamed at his failure that he jumped in after Nanahuatzin and became the moon, destined to follow Nanahuatzin's sun through the sky.

Above: *Tlaloc, ruler of the third sun and the Aztec god of rain, is depicted in this detail of a replica of a fresco dating from the Teotihuacan civilization of the 3rd to 8th centuries* A.D. *Able to bring both nourishing rain or devastating drought, Tlaloc was one of the most powerful Aztec deities.*

Aztec Calendars

The Aztecs developed complex calendars for predicting seasonal changes, which was vitally important to farming. They also used the calendars to forecast sacred periods of danger.

In the National Museum of Anthropology in Mexico City stands the Sun Stone, or Aztec calendar, a large round stone covered with intricate carvings. In the center of the stone is an image of Nahui Ollin, the current sun, which was created when the god Nanahuatzin threw himself into the fire. Around him are the names of the four earlier suns, as told in "The Five Suns" myth (see page 38).

The Aztecs were among the most accomplished astronomers of Mesoamerica. They used the day and night skies as the basis for two methods of keeping track of the year and therefore anticipating the change of seasons.

The first, based on a Mayan ritual calendar, had a 260-day cycle, made up of units of 20 consecutive days. Each 20-day period was named for a deity and combined with numbers from 1 to 13. A whole cycle would be complete when every name and number combination, such as Tlaloc 3 or Huitzilopochtli 12, had passed.

The second type of calendar was based on the solar year and lasted for 365 days. It was made up of 18 periods of 20 days, with five spare days at the end of the year.

AVOIDING DESTRUCTION

Besides marking the passage of time, the calendars, which were read counterclockwise, were meant to predict sacred and dangerous periods. The most dangerous period for the Aztecs was thought to occur every 52 years, when the two calendars aligned.

Above: *The Aztec Sun Stone, which once stood on the Great Pyramid at Tenochtitlán, is not a proper calendar but is thought by many archaeologists to represent the five mythic world creations, or suns, as in "The Five Suns." The carving in the center is thought to be the face of the sun.*

Left: *This carving represents the bundle of 52 sticks that would be bound together and then burned during a solemn ritual held every 52 years. The Aztecs hoped that the ritual would convince the gods to save the world.*

The Aztecs believed that at the end of each of these long cycles the world was threatened with destruction. Therefore, it was important to mark the end of a 52-year period with certain rituals that involved the whole community. The Aztecs believed that if these rituals were not followed correctly there was always the danger of upsetting the gods, who might then destroy everything.

To avoid angering the gods, each cycle ended with a New Fire Ceremony. For five days before the end of the cycle altar fires were extinguished, and people destroyed their furniture and possessions as

they mourned the passing of the old cycle and perhaps even the world.

On the last day of the cycle priests would travel to the Hill of the Star, a crater in the Valley of Mexico, to wait for the Pleiades stars, or Seven Sisters, to appear in the night sky. If the stars were visible then the world would continue. To celebrate, the priests would light a fire in the body of a dead animal from which all other fires would be lit. Sacrifices, feasting, and the renovating of people's possessions and houses would follow.

Below: *The ancient pyramids of the Sun (right) and the Moon (left) at the city of Teotihuacan, were inspirations to the Aztecs. The city is over 2,000 years old and 33 miles (50 km) from Tenochtitlán. The Aztecs also held a great reverence for the sky.*

The Departure of Quetzalcoatl

The myth of Tezcatlipoca's victory over Quetzalcoatl is symbolic of the historic victory, long before the Aztecs, of the aggressive Toltec culture over the peaceful Teotihuacans.

WHEN QUETZALCOATL RULED over the Toltecs they were happy. The Toltecs were skilled at crafts and Tula, their capital city, grew rich. As the years passed Quetzalcoatl grew old and slightly ill. It was during this time that Tezcatlipoca, who had been waiting for an opportunity to get rid of his rival Quetzalcoatl, began his evil tricks.

Disguised as an old man, Tezcatlipoca presented himself at the royal palace in Tula and told the guards he had medicine for their ruler. Quetzalcoatl received the old man, but when he was offered the medicine he recognized Tezcatlipoca. Discovered, Tezcatlipoca fled.

Within a few days Tezcatlipoca returned to Tula, this time disguised as a seller of green chilies. He stood near the palace until Quetzalcoatl's daughter noticed him. On first sight she fell passionately in love with the chili seller. She pleaded with her father to let her marry him, and not realizing that the chili seller was really Tezcatlipoca, Quetzalcoatl consented.

Following the marriage Tezcatlipoca, as the chili seller, started to exert a strong power over the Toltecs, causing a series of disasters. First he hypnotized a large group of people with his singing, then beating a drum faster and faster led the people to dance over the edge of a ravine, where they were turned into stones.

Other disasters followed until one day he caused all the food in Tula to rot. Following this Tezcatlipoca disguised himself as an old woman and started to roast fresh corn. Lured by the smell, the remaining Toltecs rushed to the old woman's house where the corn was roasting. As soon as they entered Tezcatlipoca killed them.

With the Toltecs dead Quetzalcoatl realized he had been beaten by Tezcatlipoca and knew that the time had come for him to leave Tula. He set fire to the city and buried his silver and gold. Then he ordered all the brightly colored birds to fly away and changed the cacao trees into useless cacti. When he left, Quetzalcoatl was accompanied by his faithful dwarfs and hunchbacks.

Together Quetzalcoatl and his entourage walked many miles toward the east and when anyone asked him where he was going he replied, "I am going to learn."

But Tezcatlipoca was not satisfied with expelling Quetzalcoatl from Tula and continued

Above: *Quetzalcoatl, represented here as a plumed serpent, was originally a Teotihuacan god. Sometime between the 3rd and 8th centuries A.D., the Teotihuacans built a pyramid, on which this carving is found, dedicated to the peaceful god. Tezcatlipoca was a Toltec god. The Toltecs dominated the Teotihuacans from the 9th century on.*

to chase him, causing him more misery. As Quetzalcoatl and his group climbed the snowy slopes of the volcanoes of Popocatepetl and Ixtaccihuatl, all his companions died of cold and Quetzalcoatl was left alone.

When the lonely and defeated Quetzalcoatl finally reached the sea he used the only magical power he had left and made a raft out of serpents. Stepping onto the raft of serpents, Quetzalcoatl sailed away to an unknown destination.

The Fall of the Aztec Empire

Ruthless and fearsome, the Aztec empire ruled neighboring cultures with a heavy hand. Yet within a matter of months, a small band of Spanish soldiers destroyed the mighty empire.

The belief that the mythical god Quetzalcoatl would return played a crucial role in the downfall of the Aztec empire. Since 1502, when Montezuma II was crowned ruler of the Aztecs, there had been a series of strange omens. These included a comet racing across the night sky and soothsayers having visions of the destruction of the Aztec capital, Tenochtitlán.

Then in April 1519 a white, bearded warrior wearing a hat with plumed feathers anchored his ship and set up camp near modern-day Veracruz. To many throughout the empire this stranger was the Toltec god Quetzalcoatl — often represented as a plumed serpent — returning to reclaim his place as ruler of the Toltecs and Aztecs.

In fact, the white, bearded warrior was the conquistador Hernando Cortés. The conquistadores were leaders of the Spanish conquest of the New World in the 16th century. They had two motives, to expand Spanish territories and to find gold.

Montezuma II, in an attempt to persuade Cortés/Quetzalcoatl to stay away from Tenochtitlán, sent gifts of jewels, gold, and human sacrifices. But Cortés, who learned that he had been mistaken for Quetzalcoatl, was determined to take advantage of the opportunity. He began marching his troops toward the Aztec capital.

BESIEGING TENOCHTITLÁN

Although he had only a few hundred soldiers, compared to the millions of Aztecs, Cortés did have several advantages. Unlike the Aztecs, the conquistadores had horses, guns, and

Above: *Hernando Cortés, the Spanish conquistador, began the transformation of Mesoamerica into a Spanish colony by first destroying the Aztec empire.*

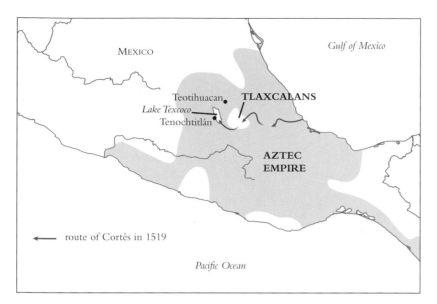

when during an Aztec uprising, the emperor was killed either by his own warriors or strangled by the Spanish. Although Cortés and his soldiers were forced to flee, they returned a year later with a stronger army and besieged the city for many months until it finally surrendered in August 1521.

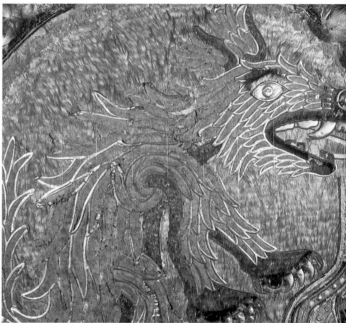

well-trained fighters. Also, during his march to Tenochtitlán he formed alliances with many Mesoamerican tribes, such as the Tlaxcalans, who were hostile toward the Aztecs.

When the Spanish arrived at Tenochtitlán on November 8, 1519, they were welcomed as guests but quickly betrayed the Aztec emperor's trust by taking him prisoner. For the next few months Cortés ruled the Aztecs through the captive Montezuma, until July 1520,

Above: *The Aztec empire at the time of the arrival of the conquistadores.*

Right: *This shield made of feathers and used in rituals was one of the many Aztec treasures Cortés sent to Spain.*

The End of the Aztecs

The Spanish did not just bring an end to the Aztec empire — they also unwittingly brought with them diseases to which the peoples of North and South America had no natural immunity. During the hundred years following the defeat of Tenochtitlán, the Aztec population fell from an estimated 12 million to a few hundred thousand. This dramatic decrease was due mostly to diseases such as smallpox, measles, and typhus.

For those Aztecs who survived the epidemics, the Spanish refused to allow them to practice their religion or customs in an attempt to Europeanize them. Also many Aztecs married Spanish settlers, and within several generations the Aztecs ceased to be a distinct people.

Glossary

ayllu An Inca social group to which members were loyal. Every member of the Inca empire belonged to an *ayllu*.

Cavillaca In an Inca myth, a woman who fled to the sea when she discovered that the spirit **Coniraya Viracocha** was the father of her baby. When she reached the sea she and her baby turned into rocks.

Chac The Mayan name for the god **Tlaloc**.

Chalchiuhtlicue The wife of the god **Tlaloc**. In an Aztec myth she ruled over the fourth world, known as the Sun of Water.

Chichén Itzá One of the major Mayan cities in the Yucatán.

codex An ancient manuscript, usually with illustrated pages.

Coniraya Viracocha An Inca spirit who tricked a beautiful woman into having his child. His actions delivered fish to the sea.

conquistador Meaning "one that conquers," a leader of Spanish troops in the conquest of **Mesoamerica** and Peru.

Cortés, Hernando or **Hernán** Born in 1485 and died in 1547, the Spanish conquistador who conquered the Aztec empire.

Coyolxauhqui The warrior goddess who tried to kill her mother, Coatlicue, and was defeated by her brother **Huitzilopochtli.**

Cuzco The capital of the Inca empire, according to legend it was founded by **Manco Capac** and his

sister **Mama Ocllo**. The ancient city is located in Peru.

floating gardens Gardens built by the Aztecs for farming; they floated atop Lake Texcoco.

Gucumatz In a Mayan myth he was a plumed serpent who along with the god **Huracan** made the corn people, ancestors of humans.

hieroglyphs A system of writing that is made up mostly of drawings or illustrations, instead of letters.

Huitzilopochtli Aztec god of war.

Hunahpu In Mayan mythology Hunahpu and his twin brother, **Xbalanque**, defeated the evil lords of **Xibalba** and destroyed the bird god **Vucub Caquix.**

Huracan The Mayan sky god who with **Gucumatz** made the corn people, the ancestors of humans.

Mama Ocllo The sister of **Manco Capac**, who with her brother founded **Cuzco**.

Manco Capac The first ruler (or Inca) of the **Quechua** speakers known as the Incas.

Mesoamerica During pre-Columbian times it was the region that spread from modern-day central Mexico to Nicaragua.

mita A tax, usually in the form of weapons, cloth, potatoes, or corn, that most members of the Inca empire were forced to pay.

Mixtecs A **Mesoamerican** civilization who were conquered by the Aztecs in the 15th century.

Montezuma II Born in 1466 and died in 1520, thought of as the last Aztec ruler. He was captured by **Cortés** and killed by either Spanish soldiers or Aztec warriors.

Nanahuatzin A sickly Aztec god who became the fifth sun, from then on known as Nahui Ollin.

New Fire Ceremony An Aztec ceremony held every 52 years to mark the end of the sacred cycle. During the ceremony the Aztecs burned all their belongings.

Olmecs The first great civilization in **Mesoamerica**, where they were dominant from 1100 to 800 B.C.

Pachacuti Inca ruler during the 15th century who greatly expanded the empire.

Pizarro, Francisco Born in 1475 and died in 1541, the Spanish explorer who conquered the Incas.

Popol Vuh A book of Mayan mythology from the 16th century.

pre-Columbian Refers to the period before the European explorer Christopher Columbus arrived in the so-called New World.

Quechua The language spoken by the Incas. Scholars generally refer to the Incas as the Quechua speakers.

Quetzalcoatl Originally a Teotihuacan deity, later adopted first by the **Toltecs** and then by the Aztecs. He was often represented as a feathered serpent.

quipu A string with knots tied in different places. The Incas used it to record information.

slash-and-burn farming
The practice of cutting down and burning forests and vegetation to make way for farmland. It was used by the Mayas in the Yucatán.

Sun Stone An ancient Aztec calendar currently housed in a museum in Mexico City.

Tecuciztecatl An Aztec god who wanted to be the fifth sun, Nahui Ollin, but instead became the moon.

Tenochtitlán The capital of the Aztec empire. The city, which lies beneath modern Mexico City, was founded in around A.D. 1325. The god **Huitzilopochtli** supposedly guided the ancient Aztecs to the site.

terrace farming The practice of carving out level terraces in the side of a steep mountain for farming.

Tezcatlipoca An Aztec deity who was usually the enemy of **Quetzalcoatl**.

tlachtli The ancient Mesoamerican ball game, which was played similarly to modern basketball or soccer.

Tlaloc Originally an **Olmec** deity who was adopted by the Aztecs as their god of rain.

Tlaltecuhtli A greedy female Aztec monster whose dismembered body became the earth.

Tlaxcalans Enemies of the Aztecs who helped **Hernando Cortés** conquer **Tenochtitlán**.

Toltecs Ancient civilization who dominated Mesoamerica during the period roughly between the eras of the **Olmecs** and the Aztecs.

Tula Ancient capital city of the **Toltec** empire.

Viracocha According to the Incas, the supreme being and the force behind all creation.

Viracocha Inca Ruler of the Inca empire in the early 15th century.

Vucub Caquix The boastful bird god of the Mayas who threatened the creation of humans.

Xbalanque The brother of the Mayan hero **Hunahpu**.

Xibalba In Mayan mythology, the kingdom of the underworld.

Xiuhcoatl A serpent of fire that was used as a weapon by the Aztec god **Huitzilopochtli** to defeat his warrior sister **Coyolxauhqui**.

Further Reading & Viewing

BOOKS

Ardagh, Philip. *History Detectives: Aztecs*. New York, NY: Peter Bedrick Books, 2000.

Baquedano, Elizabeth. *Eyewitness: Aztec, Inca, and Maya*. New York, NY: Dorling Kindersley Publishing, 2000.

Drew, David. *Early Civilization Series: Inca Life*. Hauppauge, NY: Barrons Juveniles, 2000.

McManus, Kay. *Land of the Five Suns: Looking at Aztec Myths and Legends*. Lincolnwood, IL: NTC Publishing Group, 1997.

Morgan, Nina. *Technology in the Time of the Aztecs*. Austin, TX: Raintree/Steck Vaughn, 1998.

Nicholson, Sue. *Aztecs and Incas: A Guide to the Pre-Colonized Americas in 1504*. New York, NY: Larousse Kingfisher Chambers, 2000.

VIDEOS

Great Cities of the World: Fall of the Aztec and Maya Empires. Questar, 1999.

Lost Mummies of the Inca. A&E Video, 2000.

National Geographic's Lost Kingdoms of the Maya. National Geographic, 1997.

Nova: Secrets of Lost Empires — Inca. WGBH Boston, 1997.

WEBSITES

Discovery School's A-to-Z History. http://school.discovery.com//homeworkhelp/worldbook/atozhistory

Encyclopedia Mythica: An Encyclopedia on Mythology, Folklore, and Legend. http://www.pantheon.org/mythica

Mythology Reference Link Library. http://members.aol.com/mythmstr/mythos.html

Index